CHILDREN LEARNING BOOKS

ANT

Jessica Cheong

ISBN: 9781980247937

Hi, my name is Alvin. I am an ant. Do you want to know some fun facts about me?

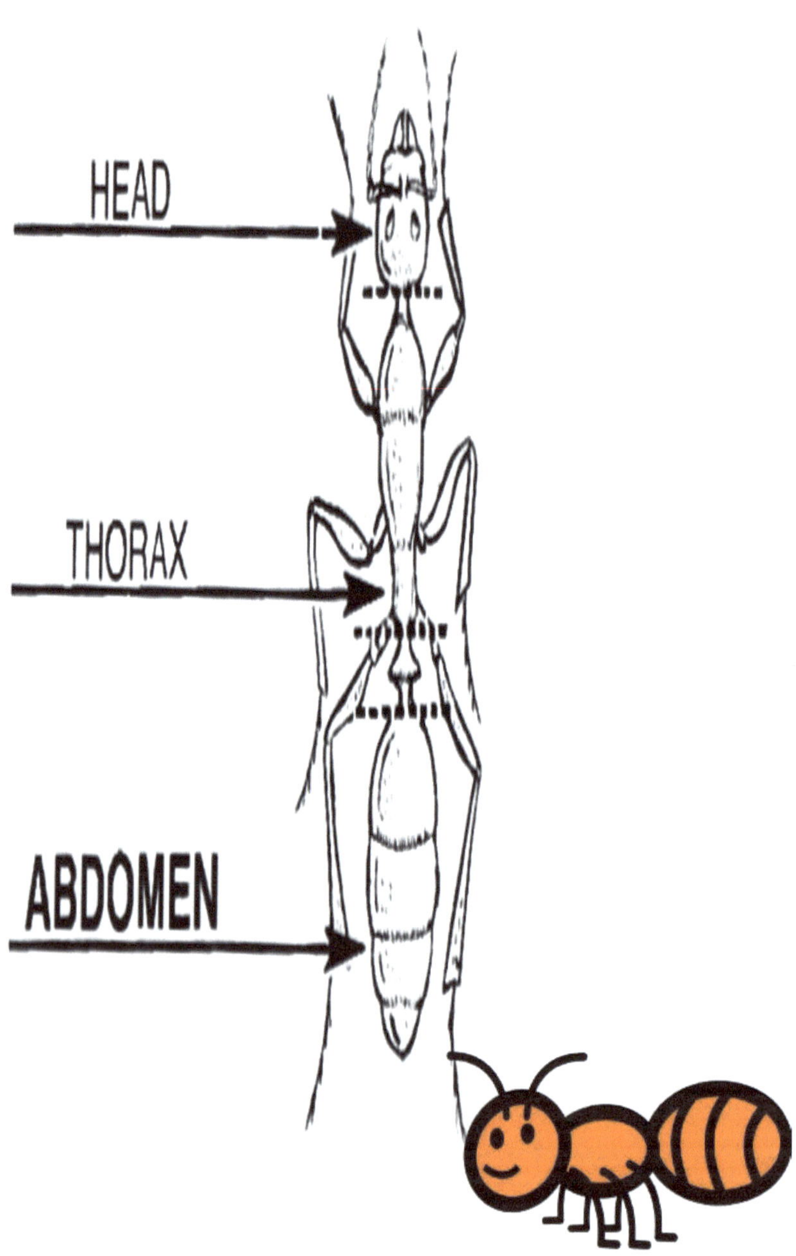

HEAD
THORAX
ABDOMEN

My body is divided into three main parts, head, thorax and abdomen.

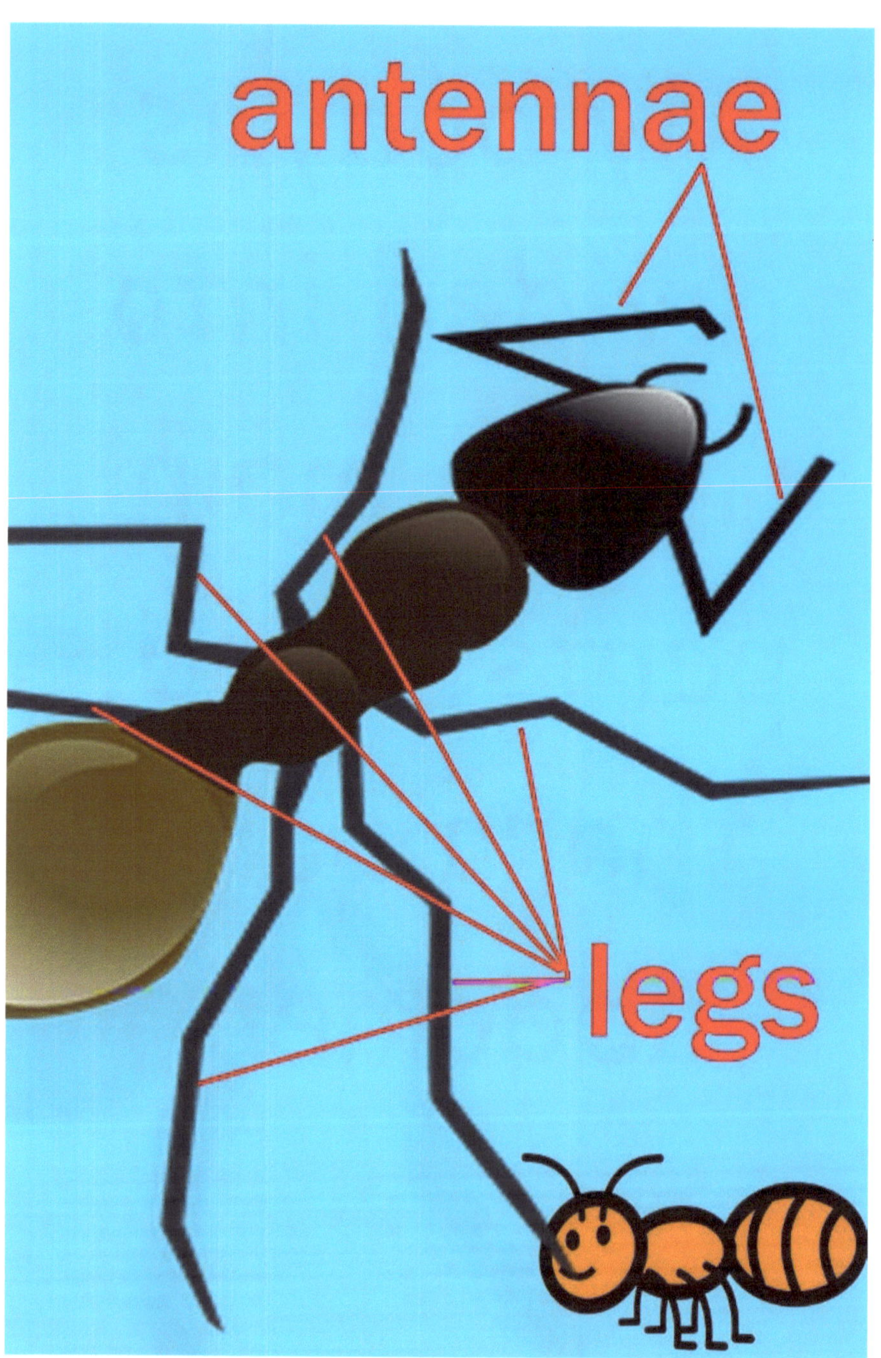

antennae
legs

I have six legs
that attached
to my thorax,
and two
antennae on
my head.

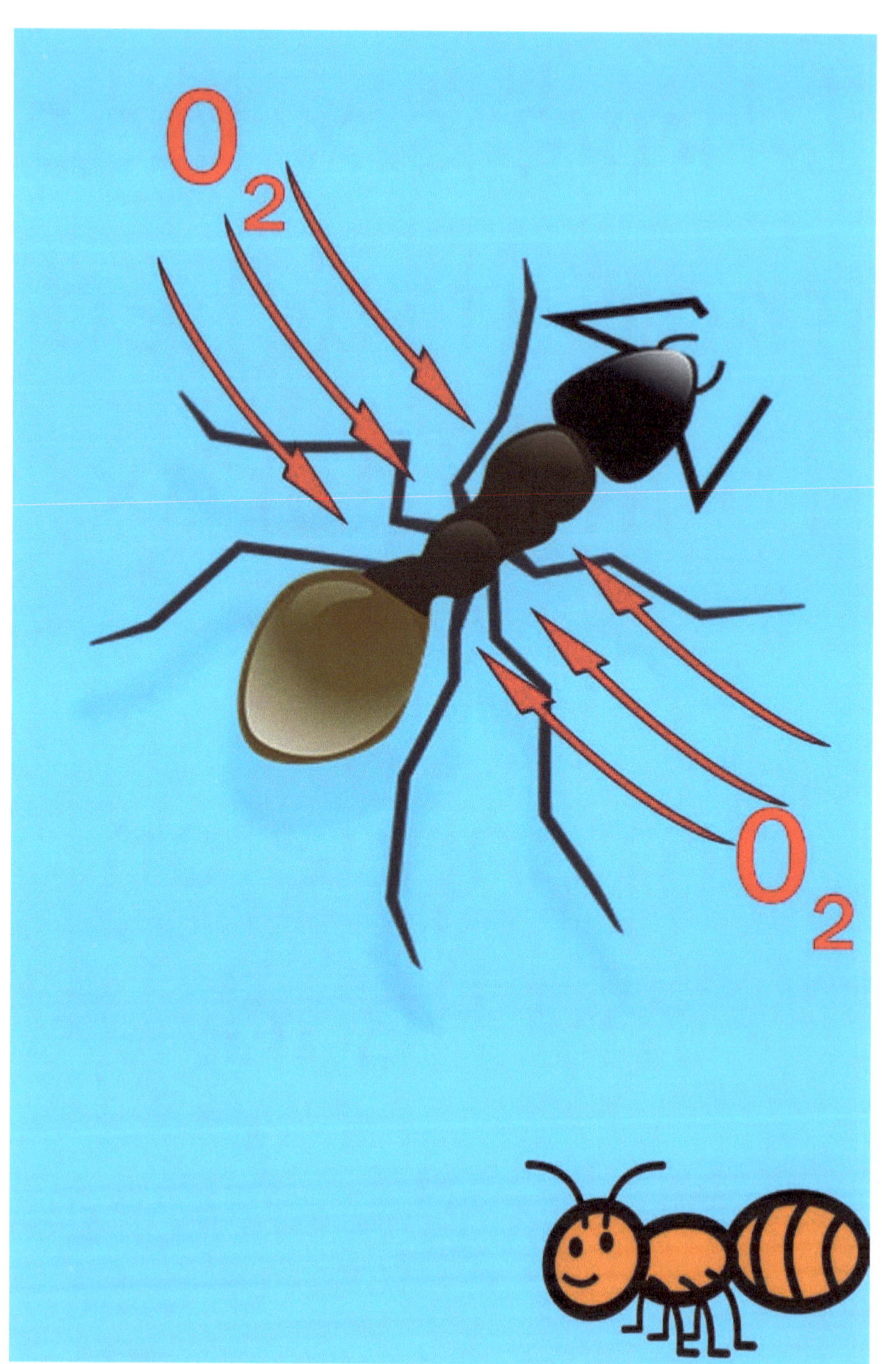

O2
O2

I don't have lungs. Oxygen enters through tiny holes all over the body.

I don't have
ears. Ants
"hear" by
feeling
vibrations in
the ground
through my
feet.

I can lift 20 times my own body weight.

Do you know how many species of ant in this world? There are more than 10,000 known ant species around the world.

10,000,000,000,000,000

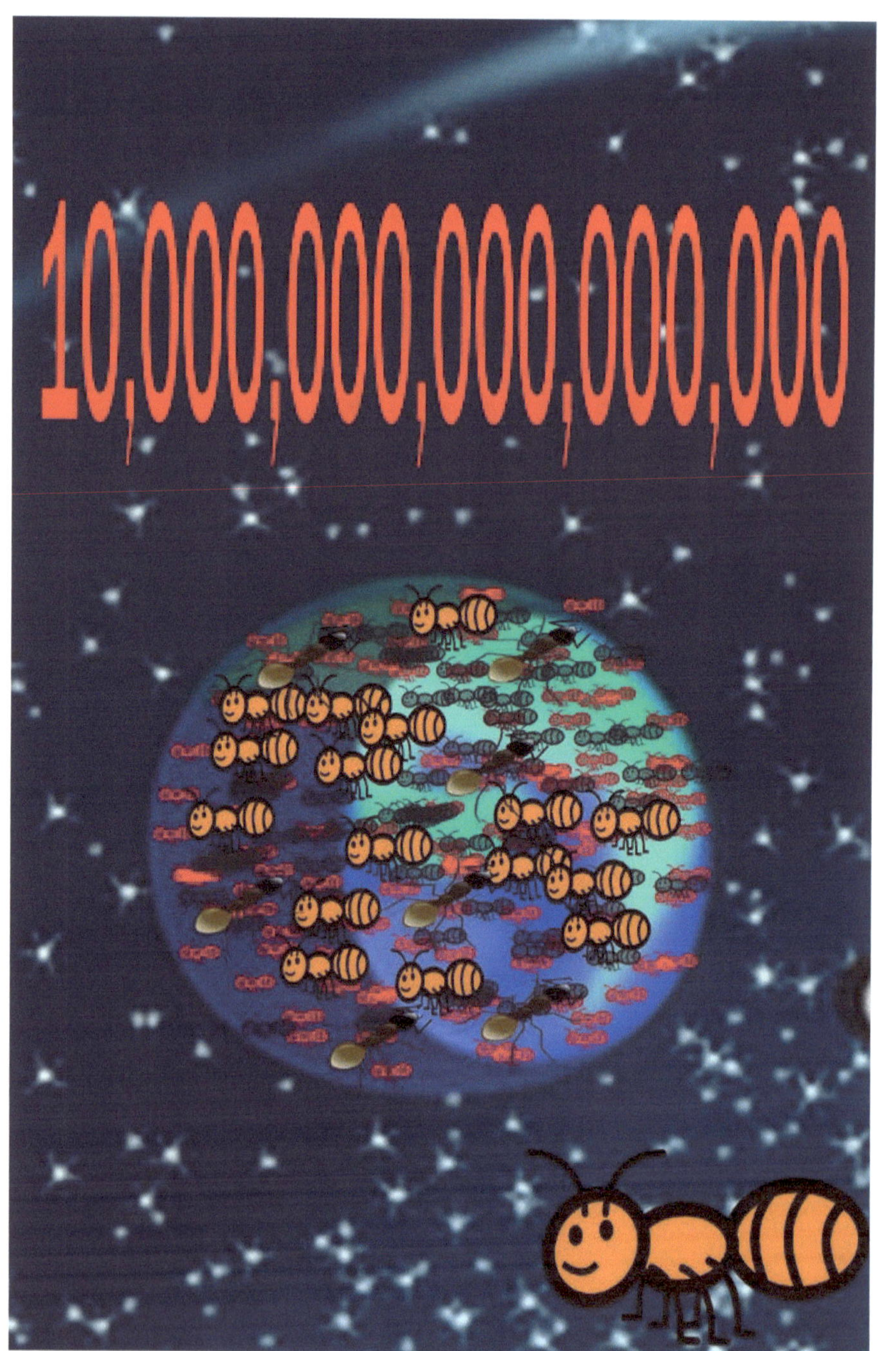

It estimated that the total number of ants alive in the world at any one time is between one and ten quadrillion (10,000,000,000,000,000).

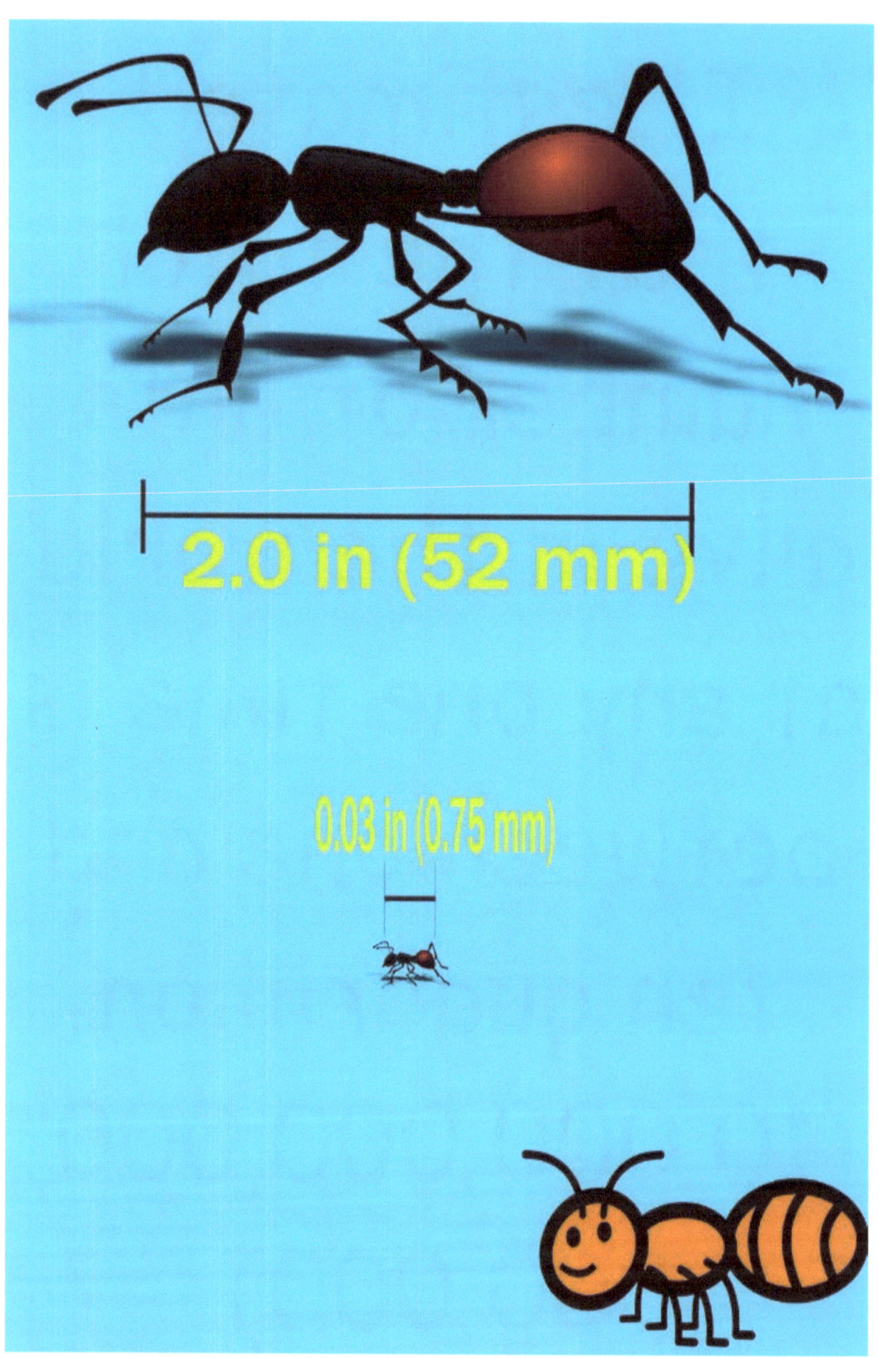

2.0 in (52 mm)
0.03 in (0.75 mm)

Ant species
range in size
from 0.75mm
to 52mm
(0.03in -
2.0in).

We are social insects, we love to live in big colonies.

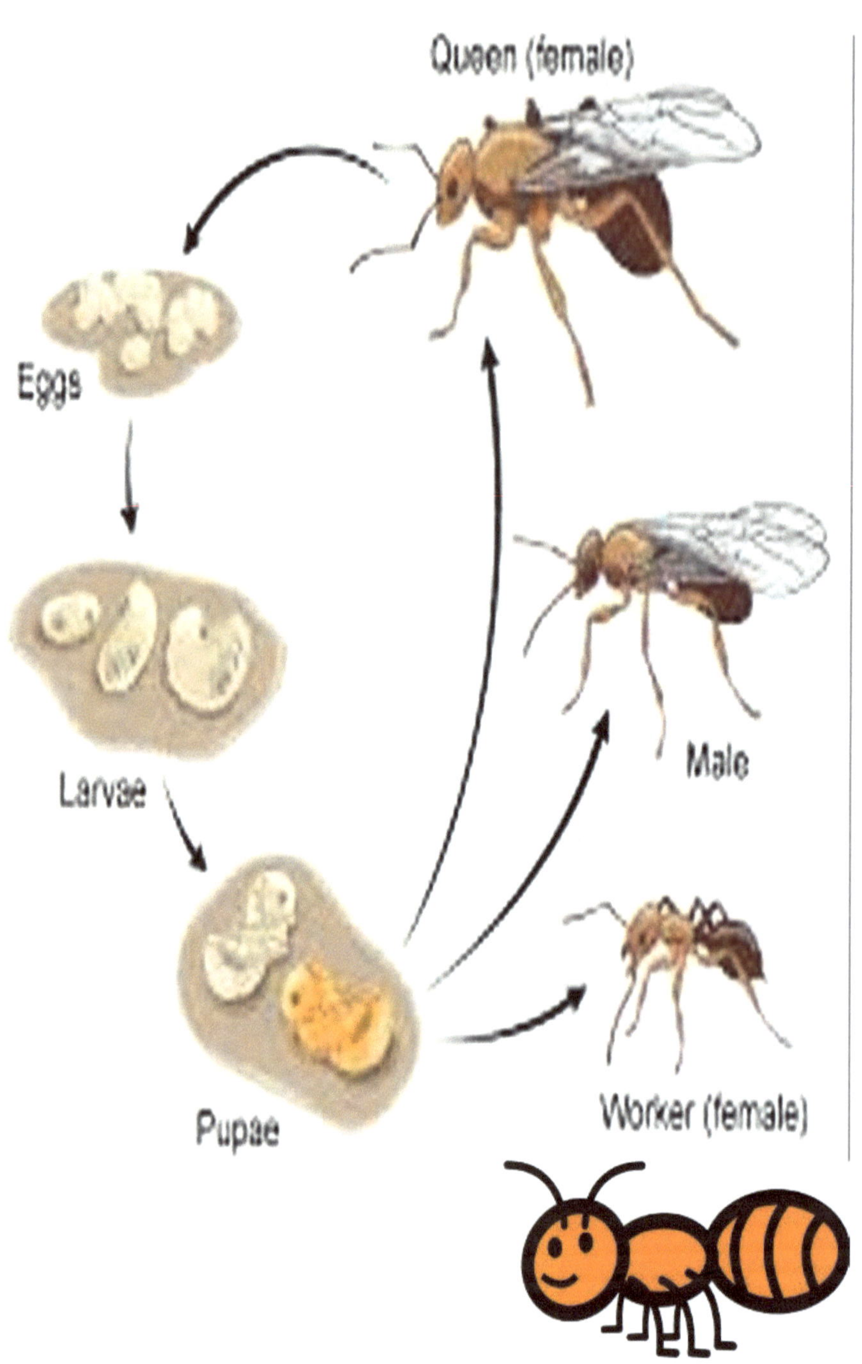

Queen (female)
Eggs
Larvae
Pupae
Male
Worker (female)

There are three kinds of ants in a colony: The queen, the workers, and males.

Ant colonies also have soldier ants that protect the queen, defend the colony, gather or kill food, and attack enemy colonies in search for food and nesting space.

700 ft (200 metres)

Worker ants can travel up to 200 meters (700 ft) from their nest and find their way back to the colony by following scent trails left by others.

Thank You

I hope you enjoy reading this book. Please leave an honest review on Amazon.

My Books

All my books are available in Amazon Kindle and Paperback. They are all enrolled in Kindle Unlimited and Kindle Owners' Lending Library.

You can visit my author page:

http://www.amazon.com/author/jessicacheong

Children Story Books:

1. **Children Story Books – Ella's Day at Kindergarten**
   Kindle ASIN: B075VTPNVV
   Paperback ASIN: 1549813471
   Paperback ISBN: 9781549813474

2. **Children Story Books – Ella At The Beach**
   Kindle ASIN: B077QJL5VF
   Paperback ASIN: 1973376520
   Paperback ISBN: 9781973376521

Children Learning Books:

1. **Animals in Alphabets and Their Habitats**
   Kindle ASIN: B06XDLML3L
   Paperback ASIN: 1520746725
   Paperback ISBN: 9781520746722

2. **Children Learning Books – Ant**
   Kindle ASIN: B079Q8V57J
   Paperback ASIN: 1980247935
   Paperback ISBN: 9781980247937

3. **Children Learning Books – Alligator**
   Kindle ASIN: B07N2B4YNY
   Paperback ASIN: 1795003626
   Paperback ISBN: 9781795003629

www.ingramcontent.com/pod-product-compliance
Lightning Source LLC
Chambersburg PA
CBHW041804260726
48664CB00034B/325